CREATE A GREAT BRAND
NEW LIFE

I0152413

CREATE A GREAT BRAND NEW LIFE

ANDREIA POSTON

Brett Lark

Brett Lark LLC

Copyright © 2018 Andreia Poston

The moral right of the author has been asserted.

All rights reserved.
No part of this publication may be reproduced, stored in a retrieval system, or transmitted, in any form or by any means, without the prior permission in writing of the publisher, nor be otherwise circulated in any form of binding or cover other than that in which it is published and without a similar condition including this condition being imposed on the subsequent purchaser.

Published by Brett Lark LLC

Edited by Gwyn Abbott

ISBN 978-0-9967704-4-6

Typesetting services by BOOKOW.COM

DEDICATION

This book is dedicated to my parents, who raised me by always teaching me great values. I am very thankful for all their hard work raising four daughters in the North of Brazil. My mother, Aldenice Rosa Barros, has been a great influence in my life. There is no compromising when the subject is to do what is right, even if it takes much more work. She taught me how to be strong and how to truly care about others. My father, Antonio Azevedo Barros, taught me to always find a way to achieve my dreams, to be compassionate towards others, and to give even when we did not have much. I further dedicate this book to Lee Harry Poston, who is always very supportive of me, my dreams, and our family. Lee has been a strong ally, my best friend, and my husband. He has brought so much positivity into my life. I dedicate this book to my children, Lucas Barros Poston and Luana Rosa Poston, who I hope to teach how to build a solid foundation so that they can grow and continue to be amazing human beings with great hearts and beautiful creative minds. I want to teach them to always have God in their lives every step of the way. I also want to thank all of my teachers throughout this life and further. Special thanks to all teachers around the world for the work they do on a daily basis. A great big thank you to all my aunts and uncles who were also very influential in my upbringing. A huge thank you to Brett Lark, a wonderful friend and great supporter of my work.

Finally, I would like to thank all of my friends, colleagues, and supporters. You know who you are! Thank you very much.

Many thanks to all my extended family around the world, to all my brothers and sisters, and to the friends that have truly become family to me.

I am truly blessed by all the amazing people that are part of my life in some way, shape, or form. You have all helped me grow, and I hope this book will serve you in your own mission to create a great brand new life and live it every day.

CONTENTS

INTRODUCTION

God is my primary source of energy and redemption. I have learned how to appreciate God as the loving creator who guides me throughout my life experiences and to accept his love. Allow God to be your primary source of energy and, even during your weakest moments, you will find peace and you will feel strong again. Your relationship with God and Jesus Christ gives you the strength to allow yourself to be forgiven and to forgive others, ultimately providing a lighter life; so, forgive whoever has hurt you so that you don't uphold your pain and their pain any longer. True forgiveness is an important step towards creating a great brand new life. When you forgive, you liberate yourself from pain and sad or hurtful memories that really do not bring you anything good. I understand we may feel apprehensive about forgiving someone only to be hurt again to the same extent. However, living in fear is not a good way of living either.

When you forgive someone, it is okay to teach the other person new and acceptable ways to behave around you. After you forgive the wrong or hurtful behavior, lift up your standards by *either* explaining to the person the moment it happens again that this behavior is what caused the separation in the first place and kindly asking for it to stop *or* having a conversation with the person at a later time to try to learn what is the root of the behavior and fix the cause not the symptom. By doing this, you will be helping yourself greatly, but best of all you could also be helping the other person with a breakthrough. I understand there are extreme cases when, even after forgiving someone, distance is necessary. Yet the act of forgiveness is for you more than anyone else. Take the appropriate measures to forgive others and do not hold grudges; that is absolutely not healthy at all.

Write out a declaration of forgiveness for yourself. You may even read it out loud to yourself in front of a mirror. Every breath you take carries a new chance to do better, to be better. Learn quickly, do better even faster, and keep a positive upward motion in all aspects of your life. I wrote my own declaration of forgiveness based on all the things I felt guilty about. There were so many things I wished I could have done differently and I used to carry that baggage around with me, that heavy weight of guilt and meaningless occurrences from the past. Once I wrote the declaration of forgiveness, I read it out loud. I even went for a run afterwards, and it felt great! Sometimes we are locked in prisons we have the key to get out of. We must take a step and do something about it. Do it now. Start where you are at and use the tools and knowledge you do have to build upon that. Action and Inaction both carry powers. The power of action is intended movement and the power of inaction is pulling pressure, a lot of times taking us in the direction we do not want to go. Gravity pulls.

Decide today to change your life for the better by making choices that enhance your life. Life is made up of small pieces; I call them recipe pieces. If you want a certain result, you can either consciously or unconsciously follow the recipe in order to attain the desired outcome. Become conscious about the choices you are making and make a realistic assessment of what the consequences of those choices will be. Think about the outcome you wish to accomplish and make the choices that will move your closer to this outcome. If it moves you closer, do more of it; if not, choose a different route. Please keep in mind that each stage of this process takes a level of effort towards self-discovery. Here are some of the action packets, or recipe pieces, that I have found to be extremely helpful during these moments…

TAKE CONTROL OF YOUR THOUGHTS

TAKE control of your mind. You must train your mind to stay at high peak performance at all times. It takes real training for that to happen and this is an important exercise because your thoughts are driving your life in many ways. With your mind, you have the power to create, to imagine, to dream, to build, and also to intentionally or unintentionally sabotage your own dreams. You can use your mind to discover who you really are within yourself and to help create the material world in which you can choose to live and remain. On the other hand, if you are not in control of your own mind then the world and other worldly influences may be: trends, news, television in general, people you associate with, etc.

I have personally experienced and created pathways for myself to break certain patterns and to start living life on my own terms, free of unwanted guilt and filled with more personalized choices, based on my values and reasons that make sense to me. Regardless of where the crowd is going, I generally choose the opposite way, or at least question the direction. I am thinking before taking the first, or even the second, step to make sure it makes sense to me, if that is indeed where I want to go. This is a life of freedom, of choices with consequences and also rewards. I want to live life on my own terms with the influences I consciously choose to follow, which in my case is the influence of God. God is the main creator and the main source of energy in my personal life, and all other influences must be in alignment with that for me.

What is the driving force in your own life? What values do you live by on a daily basis? Who are you? When did you set that identity for yourself? Do you want to change? What do you want to change and why? Will it be challenging at first? Will it create a long lasting, positive change? Why is it worth it for you to try it? What is at stake? Are you afraid? What are you afraid of? Why? Are you too comfortable to change? Life may not be too bad, but not amazing either. What will it take for you to start taking your life beyond your comfort zone, to reach the level of sound happiness and excitement not only when big things happen but every day for the rest of your life? It is possible. You can do it. Start by clearing your mind first; clarity is key for high achievement in life. I will take you through my own breakthroughs, struggles, and successes in my fight for a mind that is clear, free, positive, and strong. I hope you find it useful and I hope my insights will serve you on your own journey to create a great brand new life, starting today.

As I am going through my day, there are over a million things I could easily get distracted with that pull me away from my own focus. If I allow that to happen often, then I could get in the habit of having a pivot-oriented mind that can hardly ever complete one full thought at a time. If you are not in control of your own mind, then someone else's influence is. For instance, the songs you hear playing over and over again are potentially pre-programing certain behaviors that you may later develop. When you become aware of how music influences you, try becoming more selective of the times during your day that you listen to certain songs; pay special attention to the lyrics of the songs you listen to and choose wisely; and try to distinguish between the rhythm of the song and its effects to your body and bodily sensations and the song's real intent. First of all, start by being selective about the songs you listen to early in the morning on your way to work or school, or just at home. Think of songs as programing tools from an outside source. You must choose the source and incorporate it with the purpose you want to reach by listening to it. Secondly, choose the predominant thoughts that cross through your mind wisely, only allowing the ones that build you up and make you feel stronger, happier, and more positive. Become the commander in chief of your own mind.

Look beyond the simple pleasure of listening to a fun beat. Start asking yourself what you really expect to gain from listening to certain songs and make the appropriate selection according to the real feelings you wish to create. Focus your mind towards that great, brand new, fun, happy, and fulfilling life you have always wanted. I enjoy listening to calm, inspirational songs in the mornings because it gives me a sense of tranquility. My most successful and strong days start with a 5:00am wake-up call, followed by reading The Bible, and doing my morning high-intensity workout for an hour. Then I listen to calm and inspirational songs while getting ready for the day. In my mind, I am generally thinking of any good, positive aspects of life that I am thankful for. In life, it is essential to spend the most energy feeding the positive aspects on a daily basis because you will get more of what you focus on.

Prior to adhering to this way of thinking and choosing to behave this way, I used to allow my mind to replay negative thoughts and I would feel so much guilt within me. I felt horrible. I used to allow my mind to play something negative so many times. I used to be sad for days. I felt completely vulnerable and hurt by the simplest things. I could not believe how the world, or how people, could be so hurtful, mean, and unfair. How could someone make me feel so bad? One day, I got tired of it and I realized I was the commander in chief of my mind. I found out the moment I stopped focusing, thinking, and drilling deep into what was making me sad, I could actually make it stop.

For someone with a clear mind, this is a simple process. But when you are creating your own pathways to live with a mind that is free from all the guilt, mistakes, problems and influences, mistreatments, forms of abuse, traumas and so on, it is a different game. That is why two people may experience similar problems and take completely different viewpoints about what happened, what they felt, and how that experience either enhanced or destroyed their lives. The majority of the time, each person will take a totally different perspective based on their state of mind, life experiences, and different approaches to life.

I used to focus on my own problems, worries, sense of loss, lack of resources, and broken heart; therefore, I used to feel pain, depression, and hurt. When I intentionally focused on reading, learning, studying, and exercising, I felt empowered and in control. Once the first step is taken, repetition is key until it becomes natural to expel self-destructive patterns from your mind. That is phase one of the training process.

I remember several occasions when my mind felt like a big jungle of tangled up problems and random thoughts entrapping me. My mind felt so cluttered at times that I just wanted get out of that mess, almost like a prisoner in my own body. The more I tried to get out, the more tangled up it got. What we see on the outside is a reflection of what is going on inside. During those times of mind clutter, I could not see the brightness of the days or really appreciate anything positive in my life. I felt like I was carrying the weight of the world on my shoulders. Needless to say, the exhaustion of being in that state was daunting. Yes, it was all in my mind; therefore, it was and it felt real to me. When you reset yourself to find a way out, even during the darkest moments, you can find a way. I had to believe there was a better way to live, and I allowed a light bulb to suddenly turn on inside me. I knew, since the problem was on the inside, that was the place I had to address first and foremost. What could I possibly do to change the way I was feeling? I kept asking myself questions like that.

One of the biggest lessons I learned was to fix myself first and look for new habits to break old patterns in order to help my thought process. Instead of expecting everything around me to change, I had to expect that from myself first. It worked. It still works to this day. To this day, I ask what I can change within me to attract different things into my life. What do I need to do more or less of to change certain results that I am getting now? What books will I have to read? How many hours will I have to train to get that result I want? Why is it important that I achieve it? Is it meaningful enough that it will drive me even when I am exhausted? If it is, then I do the work. I have heard before that success is a science and there are many different formulas out there. It is worth finding out what formula—what recipe—works for you to implement it, not for a day or two but all the way until you reach the desired result. I am not saying it is easy. I am saying it is possible and, on the journey, you may find other dreams and inspire other people to find their dreams too.

It is fun to explore a conversation and see where it could end up. We can have a conversation within ourselves, navigating through our thoughts for fun at times. I call it the "spider web effect" of a thought that gets carried over into many directions. This only becomes an issue when it becomes habitual not to complete one train of thought at a time. When having a conversation, take mental notes to help you complete your own thoughts and express them accordingly. You may record the topic, and make notes later on too, so as to extract the points that are circulating in the mind and transform them into focus points you can actually look at, review, and use later in life. Be moved by purpose. Everything in nature serves a purpose.

If a thought keeps circulating through your mind, then you can either carry it through until you figure out the outcome you wish to reach, or, if it is not worthwhile, you can expel that thought purposefully and substitute it immediately with something else. Do this enough times and you will be able to control what thoughts are predominantly in your mind because mind clutter is a real problem. Choose your thoughts carefully and expel the unwanted ones quickly. Our brain is an awesome research mechanism that will locate the problem and will also, if guided properly, find great solutions. You just have to ask different questions until you get the answer you need to get up and move.

It is important to view what needs improvement in your life with a growth-enhancing frame of mind. Be realistic about the areas of concern. Identify the challenges and immediately think of ways to make things better, instead of just delving into the issue or problem. Declare a war against anything that makes you feel sad or down and get to the root of it. Identify what creates sad emotions and be conscious about what you are thinking when those negative emotions occur. Refocus your attention to what would be the solution to the problem and build upon that. Exercise your mind by putting lots of resistance against those adverse thoughts, over and over again, until they no longer have any power over you. In other words, become emotionally fit.

The meanings I used to give to certain experiences I had were disempowering and quite self-destructive. If a relationship did not work out in

7

the way I imagined it, I used to blame myself for everything when, in reality, I could have given another meaning to it, such as: "Maybe the timing wasn't right" or "This person was not the right one for me" or "There is someone else even better waiting for me." Those meanings are far more uplifting than thinking "I was not good enough" or "He was the one, the only one" or "I lost."

I think back to some of the most traumatic experiences in my life, such as the deaths of close family and friends. Deadly accidents that killed my cousin and aunt at different times. Tragic deaths of close friends. Instances when I was terribly mistreated and discriminated against. Suffering from verbal abuse in school, and later in life when I left school and went out into the world. No wonder, when we reach adulthood, it is so much harder to be the kind, loving, and full of dreams as we human beings were meant to be. We experience so much suffering, mistreatment, hurt, disappointment, etc. Nonetheless, just because it is more difficult does not make it impossible, unless we let it be so. When those things happened to me, I used to watch my life as if it were a movie, separating the events that happened outside of me from what was really going on within me. You get to control how events affect you, and what meaning you live with afterwards. When it came to the deaths of relatives, I felt a strange sense of loss given the fact that I would not see them again during my next visit home. I thought about how it must have felt during their last few hours. Then I thought of their lives, and how life in general is sensitive to death, and that at some unknown moment it will also happen to all of us.

When adverse events happen in our lives, we have to ensure that we are intentionally applying constructive meanings that will allow us to get up and become stronger each and every time. The events of our lives are not going to always turn out exactly how we would have anticipated.

However, we must believe in the overall outcome for a reason, and we can either win or learn from it. Knowing the direction that you are going, staying true to your values, and moving towards your biggest dreams is the right way to go. Do not allow anything, or anyone, to take you out of this direction for good. Even if you bounce a little to the left and a little to the right, trace your way back and soon nothing and no one will to move you away, push you back, or have any power over you.

Further identify the beliefs you have about yourself and watch out for the thoughts embedded in the background of your mind. There is a section in our brains responsible for linking the nervous system, which is a network of nerves and cells that carry messages from the brain and spinal cord to various parts of the body, with the endocrine system that moves the hormones responsible for regulating physiology and behavior. This section is called the Hypothalamus. I find it intriguing that this gland is located in the central area of our brains, right above the Thalamus. One of its main functions is to maintain stability in the internal environment in the body. I feel that since our brains are firing up signals throughout our entire bodies 24/7 during our lifetime, it is crucial to watch over the environment in which these synapses are taking place. Be aware of your thoughts.

A good mind is necessary for us to create an optimal life. Remember, positive thoughts will most likely generate good feelings to the same extent that the negative thoughts will potentially produce negative emotions. Think about what builds you up emotionally. Now do that deliberately, and remember, "Your mind is a lot like a garden where weeds can grow freely but roses have to be carefully planted." Quickly root out any negative thoughts and substitute them immediately with positive ones. The mind is very much like any other muscle in your body. You must train your mind so that it executes the tasks you want it to at high peak performance. The more your train your mind, the stronger it will become.

I have a strong desire to help others; therefore, when I am not feeling at high peak performance, I quickly turn my focus to projects, whether it is writing or recording my video blogs, to enhance my belief that life is not only about me. When I turn my focus to helping other people, it automatically helps me. This gives me the strength to move forward and to keep pursuing my dreams of a meaningful life of service for my family, myself, and many others who very much need it around the world. I intend to use all the lessons I have learned, as well as the communication and writing skills I have developed, to help as many people as I can. By helping others, I am learning to contribute and I am improving myself so that I can serve better. I study, I learn, and I teach. I want every interaction in my life to lead to another positive encounter. I want to help people connect pieces that may allow them to see things clearer and encourage them to move towards their dreams. That is a powerful tool I use to build myself up emotionally. It works every time.

This is my way to fix how I am feeling internally, without masking it or trying to cover it up. Covering up emotions will just bring them to a boil, or it will reflect directly on your body and your appearance. Some ways that people mask their deeper emotions are by acting rudely or by over-eating to momentarily change their biochemistry and get that temporary feeling of contentment. However, that feeling quickly fades and brings guilt the majority of time. Other people will use alcohol or drugs, which can do harm to the body and also become an addictive corrupted channel for a temporary sense of relief. People will sometimes literally self-inflict pain on their bodies to try to take the focus away from their emotional pain, instead of getting to the root of the problem.

Acknowledging the cause, what meaning we have attached to what we feel; understanding why we have given it such a meaning; asking whether or not the meaning can be changed; and looking for a solution instead of covering up our emotions is a worthy way of living. Your emotions are guiding signals to you, so interpret them as such. Fear can be a signal for danger, anger a signal that someone invaded your personal space and overstepped boundaries, and so on. Use your emotions as signals that you must act wisely to live your life within your terms, giving and receiving the respect you deserve based on your uniqueness and the gifts you can bring into this world.

Pay close attention to your surroundings, to what types of messages the songs you are hearing over and over again are really saying. Guard your mind and do not allow outside sources to influence your decisions on a deeper level. Most important decisions are supposed to be made within, by means of prayer and meditation, using the information you have collected through God. All decisions carry consequences, so make sure you create a system that prevents you from being manipulated by outside sources and guards your mind.

REDIRECT YOUR FOCUS

By redirecting your focus, you are basically exercising your mind to move in the direction you actually want it to go. Please understand, what you focus on the most you will feel. Make sure you are focusing on what builds you up. Everyone has good qualities, but on the same token we all have some not-so-great attributes. It is our choice, deep within, to decide what we are going to pay more attention to and why, and with what objective.

What you think about with your feelings over time can really become your reality. So, what is it going to be? Bring yourself to a clarity of mind by dedicating at least 10 to 15 minutes each day to clear your mind from all the clutter and happenings of the day. Consider this time an investment in yourself. I believe in reaching within for better resourcefulness; however, outsourced imprinting is also widely used. I am very selective of any outsourced images I allow to be imprinted within my brain. This is because I prefer exploring different levels of thinking, and I like to define myself. My internal dialogue is very concise and objective. I choose what to think about, when, why, and with what objective, until I move on to the next thought. This is a skill I have developed over time; it was not always this way.

I used to allow my mind to play scenarios where I would imagine how a discussion or argument would go, and during that imaginary scenario the feelings would be so intense and real. I used to do that a lot with different scenarios and, unfortunately, the majority of them were negative. One day, I clearly noticed that if I was thinking about the negative scenario, then I would feel immediately sad; however, when I switched the focus or the thought intentionally into something else, either by including some kind of movement like shaking my head or taking a deep breath, I would feel a relief almost as if I were immediately released from the emotional pain I was feeling. The tricky part was, I was so used to nurturing those negative scenarios that it took me practicing this exercise several times until it became habitual. Nowadays, it is easier for me to recognize negative scenarios and simply throw them away by replacing them with a different thought or a better perspective.

It is great to converse with others within your own discretionary boundaries. It is amazing what listening to someone else's perspective can do to a certain thought, point of view, or idea, and it can be an enriching experience. It is also important to conduct self-analysis every once in a while, to assess where you are coming from and why you behave the way you do, and to understand the underlying reasons why you are taking certain action patterns. Finding balance lies in understanding that if you only focus on yourself, you may find yourself lost, lonely, and even depressed. God has put us here on Earth to live and collaborate with others; therefore, our focus has to be balanced and most definitely shared. I have found that the best way to bring the utmost happiness into my life is to bring an internal, well-centered type of caring focus, guided by my most unique connection to the guidance of the Creator.

PERSONAL FORMULAS

OUR personal formulas put us in the driver's seat of the feelings we create. The better you know your personal formulas, the closer you are to the result you are trying to create. Knowing your "can" and "cannot" lists, and understanding the reasons why, is an essential step prior to setting up your own personal formulas for a happy and fulfilling life. This is a systematic point of view, which amazes me because we have systems all around us: nature, government, even our body is a system of combined organs, tissues, etc. When each part works well in its capacity, systematically all goes well. Therefore, maintaining a fully-operational system of self gives you the best chance for a better result.

Getting to know yourself first, and understanding your own body, reasoning, and emotions—positive or negative—triggers progressive growth as a human being, adding on to your knowledge and enabling you to do better each time. Keep just what is eternal within you but recycle everything else to make it better each and every possible time. Some may say, "Why spend your time doing that?" I challenge them and say, "Why not?" If you can live a better life, in which you feel more fulfilled, happier, and more satisfied as you look over your amazing accomplishments, measured and judged by you on your own terms, then I say again, and again, "Why not?" The people who have reached you on a deeper level will always be with you. As in the power of remembrance when death occurs, what is truly eternal simply is! We must not fear but rather embrace the many developing and creative challenges put forth by the human race, so that we can all live a well-spent life.

Pay more attention to your own personal formulas. Using the recipe pieces, you will be able to produce the feelings you want. Ultimately, you can decide how to turn on certain feelings within yourself by focusing on the collection of facts you record within your mind. A positive match is all that is needed for you to feel good. For example, consider the love formula: someone must kiss you in a certain way, or hold your hands, or touch your hair, or speak to you in a certain manner in order for you to feel attracted to them. Please note that the love formula may be similar amongst individuals, but it is not the exact same formula across the board. Get to know your "feel-good formulas," and remember the ultimate result is to maximize your level of happiness. If you are clear about what makes you happy, then you can move more objectively towards it.

I understand that sometimes we may get stuck doing the same things and expecting different results. This usually happens because there is a deeper, underlying reason for our actions that we are trying to uncover; until that problem is solved in the open and cleared away, it is difficult to try to move past it. In the meantime, we tend to go through this cycle, even though is painful or upsetting, until we finally do something slightly different and reach a breakthrough. By consciously enacting a new formula, or action pattern, the result will be different, and hopefully more satisfactory, giving us the power to take control and break the cycle. Modeling certain action patterns that have been proven to work can be helpful. Although, if you are like me, you also have a very strong sense of originality. I want to be me. I want to trace my path and create my own experiences. The key is to find a balance in which you do not compromise who you are; however, you can still open yourself and your mind to listen and learn. At the end of the day, you can make a decision about how or if the new information you gleaned can be applicable to you, instead of just adopting a know-it-all attitude or, even worse, an attitude of indifference and inaction, none of which is helpful to the growth and self-development that serves as a foundation for you to create a great brand new life.

There is time for everything. Time to listen. Time to learn. Know your timing, be selective of what you listen to, know your whys, and expand your knowledge of yourself and your personal formulas. Be creative. Challenge yourself so you can grow. Even rocks, with the pressure of water over time, change their shapes. Create some room to make enlightening, powerful, positive changes within yourself. Ask yourself what skills you could or should develop that will transform your life. Think about getting a return on your investment, which means that the amount of time you spend learning about yourself and your personal formulas and the time you invest in developing your personal skills and talents will show up in your life. Make your commitment consistent, and always pick up where you've left off and start again.

Take this method for a test drive. Allow yourself to practice it consciously. Make notes of positive accomplishments due to knowing and exercising your formulas. I know that when I get up early in the morning, do my Bible study, go to the gym, and get my kids ready for school, my day if off to a good start! Now, I also know that the days when I hit the snooze button three times, finally turn the alarm clock off, skip the gym, wake up rushing to get everyone ready for the day, and take no time to meditate, simply do not go quite as well. Those are just some of my own feel-good rituals, or personal formulas, as I like it to call them. I apply myself on a consistent basis to keep up a strong, well-spent life.

I actually like myself even more when I do what I need to do, even when I have to push myself to do those things. Afterwards, I feel more accomplished and my self-esteem goes through the roof! In summary, know your feel-good formulas, put them into practice, make them consistent, get to know yourself on a deeper level, and start breaking through the cycles you are not satisfied with by adopting new action patterns. Changes in yourself will show in your appearance and in your overall persona and, depending on the new actions patterns you adopt, they could also show up in your body image too. Your energy levels will increase as you work towards making yourself better. The people around you will be touched by it too. It is natural that one person's change can serve to influence others around them. Be the driving force of the positive change around you.

TIME

TIME waits for no one. We are all blessed with the same number of hours each day for as long as we are alive. What we choose to do with our time has a great impact on our life and the meaning of our existence. I often feel overwhelmed with the number of activities I have to do. I have come to realize that a great way to accomplish these activities is by simply doing them little by little, one by one. Another way is to create routines that empower the completion of these daily tasks from beginning to end. I am now talking about the very basic daily tasks that a great majority of the population has to do themselves, such as laundry, cleaning, deep cleaning, washing dishes, cooking, etc. With a broader perspective, you can potentially maximize your results by focusing on outcomes instead of just activities. Do reach out to your resources, and delegate and assign activities that make sense financially to you and that will free up your time to work on the outcomes that provide the most investment return.

Time is one of your greatest assets; choose wisely how you spend it. Every morning, choose to be thankful for at least three things in your life. They can be as basic or as deep as you want. The main point is to express gratitude and to take the time to become comfortable in your own skin. Strive for perfection because you can always improve and recognize the journey is the main part of this process. The journey has to be appreciated. It renews you so that you can become brand new, with a fresh perspective and frame of mind. I always say that if your body does it for you, then you can do it for yourself too. I am fascinated by the way the body heals and adapts after a fracture or a burn. Your body works at its maximum capacity to keep you alive and finds alternative ways to work in the face of adversity.

You owe it to yourself to do so too. Remember, you are responsible. It is up to you to take action towards a better life, to focus on a constant, never-ending improvement routine. No matter what happens, you must believe that you are better, that you can be better. Life should be better and you deserve better. The power is within you to achieve that. The Bible says, "seek and you shall find." You must take this advice into serious consideration and make a habit to apply these principles in your daily life.

Appreciation will give you a sense of accomplishment on this journey. I admire "go-getters," but I admire even more the "go-getters" who appreciate what they've got! I tend to think of it this way: if you can't see, maybe you can hear, so be thankful for hearing. If you can't talk, maybe you can walk, so be thankful for walking…Remember, you want the maximum amount of energy to flow into the areas of your life that increase your levels of satisfaction, because with focus these areas will grow exponentially. Choose your focus points wisely and consciously and understand your own reasoning behind your choices. Think about what builds you up emotionally, then do that deliberately.

The way in which you consistently do this exercise will drive your emotions. Once you start seeing the results, you will be more likely to do it more often until this process becomes part of your personal routine and part of who you are. You can transform your life by first changing your thoughts and then training your mind to be strong and to always see things with a viewpoint that enriches yourself and your life. In the face of challenges, try not to look at your problems as just mere problems but rather solutions you have yet to encounter. You have more intelligence within you than you can even imagine. You must tap into that resource to live a full life.

Life can always be better. Improvement is a key factor for our happiness. How we spend our time determines how much we are growing and why we feel so alive when we are also working towards a greater goal. Working towards a goal gives us a sense of direction in life. Once that goal is achieved, we must reward ourselves and then quickly move on to the next goal. It is a fun and exciting way of living life.

I like to add the word "yet" to the end of a great deal of my sentences. When I admit I am not good at a certain aspect of my life, I like to say: "I am not good at _____ yet." As long as I am alive, I have the opportunity to improve in any aspect I choose to, and so do you. Take personal responsibility over the direction you want your life to go by saying, "I am responsible and able to love and respect myself. I can be better. I must be better. I must grow and improve as long as I have air going through my lungs. I am here to win and to learn from my life lessons, and most of all I must recognize my victories. I am strong. I am an important and crucial part of the big picture. Without the most original me, the world is simply not as good as it must be. I owe it to myself and to humanity to be the best version of myself, both for me and for the meaning of my existence." Taking a serious view of who you are, and of your responsibility, is what it means to be at your highest level of authenticity.

The broader the perspective we have of life, the smaller the window of time we find to fit it all in. Amplify your perspective by creating reasons that motivate you to get up and conquer each day. There are so many new things that can be discovered. Take the first step to reach your goal, and once you do, grab it and do not let it go. Please wake up; now is the perfect time for you to start. Read, explore, relate to other people, share your interests and your ideas, be the most original version of you—but make it very refined and sharp! You can do it. Start by asking questions, such as: "How can I become a better version of myself?" "What books would I have to read?" "What new places would I like to see to open up my horizons?"

Know your outcome is to become a better version of you. Therefore, even if something you try does not fit in initially, please understand this is a process of constant self-development. Having a sense of humor will help too because, in your quest for self-improvement, a few ideas you pursue may turn out to be quite funny. You can laugh at yourself. Sometimes I look back and laugh at some of the statements I have made, or written, or said in the past, or the ways I have behaved boldly and brashly in certain circumstances. The people of the other side of this statement will agree to that. It is more than okay to have some fun along the way, but always remember to Be Kind, Be Good, and Be Nice (BK, BG, BN).

BUILD YOUR LEGACY

Use your time to build your legacy, and a good way to do that is by having one you wish to create. What is your legacy? How do you want to be remembered?

The fun fact about that is the people who really know you will know your works because *you* took the time to know yourself first, even if someone else cannot see it. You will not tremble. You will be able to stand firm behind your opinions, your ideas, and your actions. What would it take for you to understand there is urgency in the matter of time? For me, it was thinking of life in reverse, thinking that from the moment we are conceived we start to die. Life is actually the process by which we engage in the experiences we have, and life is what we create until "life-in-reverse" happens and we die. I know this is a strong statement, but not a negative one. Whether it is 150 years from now or 100 years, even if the average life expectancy were to change, death is still inevitable.

So, I'll ask again, "What thought process would you have to engage with in order to understand that we have limited time?" Today is the best day for you to start or continue pursuing your dreams and becoming a better version of yourself. What gives me the biggest perspective of all, for me to do everything I can to the best of my abilities with all I have today and every day, is the connection with God and the belief that one day Jesus Christ will come and take his people to heaven with Him and that life will be eternal. That is the life I am living because it allows me to do good, to really care to the point that I dedicate my time to self-development and contributions to others, and I always do what I can to help as many people as possible. We all have different motivations; however, some may align. The factor that plays the biggest role is how much time you are really willing to apply so that you can work to produce the results you really want. How soon are you willing to start? What is your "why"? Your reason? Is it compelling enough to move you? If not, what would make it compelling? What is the driving force behind your actions? What would empower you to start today? Is it the time given to you on this earth? What you do with it matters. Your existence has an impact; make it a positive one. Use your time wisely and have lots of amazingness to show for it.

PHYSIOLOGY

THE way you uphold yourself says a lot about you. Take care of yourself from the inside out by watching your thoughts, protecting your mind, and managing your time properly so that you make time to do the things that are important to you. Eat for the purpose of fueling your body with the highest quality of "fuel." Eat what your body absorbs best and is able to gain the most nutrients from. This will enable you to have the energy you need to purse your dreams. Do that for yourself and for the people around you who love you and want to be around you for a long time. Eat for fuel; exercise for fitness.

Our bodies were made for movement. If you can't move anything, at least move your mind—think, read, and grow. There is always a way. Make it your mission to find yours; keep asking, researching, looking, and learning. Motion creates emotion, so move around and exercise to make your body feel more alive. Play a happy song. A few days ago, I was walking down a set of stairs at a local library and my shoes slipped. I tried holding on to the side rail, but I fell anyway. I bent my knees over as they stretched out. I thought that if only I had been in better physical condition, with more flexibility, then it could have been a clean break. I highly recommend staying on top of your fitness levels, stretching, keeping up your strength, and eating well to ensure your body composition is a healthy one.

Plus, we experience more of life when our body agrees with the type of activities we choose to do, like swimming, hiking, running, climbing, biking, or skiing. Staying physically fit opens up a lot more doors with fun opportunities to create new life experiences. My motto is "do what you can with what you have."

Improvement and growth will consequently follow if you put in the time, effort, and work. It is worth it. Do it now. Do it today. You will love yourself more for it. It will boost your self-esteem and simply make you a happier person. Look at your face closely in the mirror and pay attention to your facial expressions. Are you constantly frowning? Or do you have an angry expression? Are you happy with the lines and wrinkles you face will show over time, depending on your facial expressions? Train your face to smile more often. Hold your body with good posture and practice smiling. These are simple but effective changes in your physiology that show increased positive results within your life.

The level of intensity in my life increased according to the level of exposure I placed on myself. The more open and authentic I became, the more other people fought to have their own space and influence in my life. To enable myself to stand up for what I believed was right, I also had to strengthen my body. I aim to work out at least 4 or 5 times on a weekly basis, with high-intensity training workouts to build up my physical strength. I know that I must have enough energy to do all the work I choose to do and to be strong. By strengthening my body, I enable my body to respond to events and to emotions. I consider our bodies the armor that carries who we are within it. If treated with love, our bodies can help us experience a life with more happiness here on Earth.

The combination of all the factors discussed above can potentially determine our levels of happiness and how we uphold ourselves in times of trouble. How much something affects us physically and emotionally is often directly related to our current physical and emotional state. Life will always happen for us, around us, and to us; let's empower our bodies, minds, and souls to be receptive of the greatness that life has to offer. In times of trouble, let us have the strength and emotional preparedness to work through the challenges that may be a necessary part of our growth.

I have a strong tendency to navigate very deep within my thoughts and ideas. Physical activity helps me by bringing me back to reality. High-intensity workouts shift my focus and push out negative energy. I like a high-intensity workout, especially in the mornings, because it sets my system up the right way. It pushes me to make healthier choices throughout the day as well. My workouts currently involve a routine of warm-ups and weight lifting. I usually begin my morning workouts with muscle groups in the upper body, followed by cardio workouts in the afternoon of the same day, and vice versa. While training for the bikini competition, I increase my workouts to twice a day, four or five times a week, for 7 to 8 months. I also abstain from alcoholic drinks throughout this time. I mostly compete for the fun aspect of giving myself a reward after so much training. I do it for fun. It gives me a directional point to work towards, plus I enjoy the atmosphere and the energy.

I am usually more inclined to make a healthy blended vegetable juice after a workout instead of eating something unhealthy. One simple way to invest in my physiology for my overall physical and mental health is to try to eat a combination of natural sources of carbohydrates and fats from avocados, nuts, and lean protein. I do enjoy fish and, on occasion, chicken or beef. Water is greatly incorporated into my daily diet, as well as natural blends of cleansing and detox drinks from fresh vegetables and fruits. Home-cooked meals, soups, and stews are also a part of my diet. I do have an occasional ice-cream cone, but my kids are mostly surprised when they see me eating that because I try not to make a habit of it.

Taking care of my body allows me to live a healthier life with plenty of energy and drive. This is very crucial because you do not want to reach certain goals only to have depleted your body's energy completely because you did not pay enough attention or invest enough in yourself throughout the process. Take care of your armor and your armor will hold up strong for the optimal enjoyment of life.

RELATIONSHIPS

THIS is a very special topic for me. My life is richer because of the high quality of the relationships I have been able to establish. I take relationships very seriously. Think about it with me. The number of relationships we have in our lives ranges from the inner world to the outside world. It starts with our connection to the Creator, the daily relationship that enriches our lives. Then there is the relationship we have with ourselves: how well we balance our thoughts, how we respect ourselves, how we take care of ourselves, and ultimately how we relate to others. Next comes our relationship with our immediate family, sometimes the baseline and safe haven that must be cherished and appreciated. I have family in different parts of the world, and we do our best to stay connected. Our relationship bonds help strengthen each one of us, even from a distance.

I also have work relationships with people I currently spend more time with than my own family. A lot of us can relate to this. These relationships are important because they are tracing and molding parts of our lives due to the amount of time we spend with them and the experiences that we share. Professional relationships must be established with mutual respect, caring, and understanding. They can involve fun times too, like potlucks and birthdays, all while maintaining the professional balance of getting work tasks done in good quality and in a timely manner. Work relationships are possible and they can also make the workday more fun. The bottom line is to create empowering relationships by making each encounter a positive one. That means talking respectfully over issues, resolving problems, listening and expressing ideas, thoughts, or concerns. Not everyone will express a desire to relate to you. Remember that "no" sometimes means "not now." In the meantime, live your life on your terms and expand your horizons. It is easier to relate to others when you have common interests with the people you are trying to establish a relationship with. It takes time and work, all of which can be interesting of course.

The way we connect with other people contributes to the overall quality of our lives. We have a chance to decide what roles certain people will play depending on the meaning we give to their existence in our lives. Choose a network of people and focus on their highest qualities. Your life can be richer when you master the art of personal connection. Life is more fun when you can share certain moments and experiences with people you can relate to. Love immensely, forgive fast, and create clear boundaries and express them in a kind way. These are some of the keys to creating life-long relationships that enrich your existence as an exchange of love.

Adopt the BK, BG, BN model: Be Kind, Be Good, and Be Nice. Show appreciation for one another. Learn how to communicate your feelings to others because the quality of your communication, especially when it comes to relationships, can determine the quality of your life. Life is way more fun when you are sharing its experiences with people you care about and people who care about you. This goes for all relationships in our lives.

Mutual respect is essential as we are trying to build any relationship. Understand that there is an exchange in value when a relationship is cemented. There will be times when one person gives more than the other; however, the overall goal must be that loving and caring exchange that is uplifting and powerfully strong. Sharing knowledge, listening and talking with the intent of growing together, and sometimes simply having fun with the people you love…This is what I envision the relationships in my life to be like. This is how the relationships in my life are. I have been successfully creating this bond with a lot of amazing people, and I am happier and stronger for that.

One of my goals is to create even more powerful relationship bonds, because I believe we are here on this Earth and together we can do so much more. We can learn from one another, we can share our dreams and ideas, and one simple comment can sometimes transform the lives of others. It takes courage to take chances, but the results may be far beyond what we could have ever imagined. Even if not every relationship turns out the way we wanted it to, we can always learn from past relationships and do better next time. Never, never should we close ourselves off to deeply relating to others and developing meaningful relationships in our lives.

THE BLOCKING TECHNIQUE

I teach my children "the blocking technique." They block anything that does not add value to them because, as much as we try to limit the exposure to negative factors, the real protection comes from within and branches out. I feel that if I assist them in training their minds to bounce off the negative images, words, and behavior patterns, then they will become stronger and more assertive in the long run. I do, however, still do the best I can with what I have at hand to provide a quality, healthy lifestyle. I am really talking about those moments that happen around us and will happen more as my children grow more independently.

The blocking technique can be widely used by you as a shield to protect you and to preserve all the goodness you possess. Please note that if you are deeply connected within yourself you will know when something doesn't feel right to you. Watch for what messages your emotions are sending to you. I use the blocking technique to move my focus away from undesired information that makes its way into my mind. I am able to look right through it or to fully not hear it at all if I choose to do so.

I do that by separating what happens on the outside from what is happening inside my mind, within my thoughts and ideas. The goal is to be able to navigate between these "two worlds" quickly, to be fully present, and to respond to situations very quickly also. You determine how what happens on the outside affects you on the inside; therefore, it makes sense to pick and choose what information goes in and out respectively. Only allow what is good and useful to stay within you. Some people use the expression "garbage in, garbage out," and the blocking technique is similar to that concept. However, if you can build your shield so that you can fully block something negative, then that is even better. You do not have to see it or hear it, and your senses can be turned off on purpose to avoid those mind pollutants.

I also use this technique when relating to other people, or I see people doing it to me when I behave adversely or do something that is not usual to me. The blocking technique can also be verbalized. You can choose to ask for the behavior to be stopped, or you can simply refuse to listen to it or see it anyway. It is up to you. However, do not ignore habitual behaviors that are becoming toxic around you either. Try to have a full understanding of your threshold, and what behaviors, scenes, or actions are within your blocking levels, before taking action becomes necessary. Do a quick internal risk analysis; check the frequency of your exposure, times, variables in general, and potential consequences. How does this thing actually affect you? Are people you care about deciding to block it or to stop it? We do that automatically sometimes. This is just bringing to light a part of the process we engage with on a daily basis to make us all more conscientious and aware. Block intentionally.

Work on problems effectively with the goal of improving your overall quality of life. Please have in mind that a lot of the actions and reactions from people around you have more to do with what they are going through than with you. Learn to separate your state of mind from the disproportionate behaviors of others. People are sometimes sad, depressed, overwhelmed, angry, happy, or excited, all of which has to do with what is going on with them. Unfortunately, many people do not know how to recognize the real triggers of their emotions or the real reasons why they are feeling the way they do. The moment something happens, it all boils over. It has nothing to do with you, or with what you did or said, even if they blame you.

The blocking technique can help you separate, un-assign, or completely remove yourself from participating in someone else's meltdown, consequently making you stronger and a more helpful being in such circumstances. Because you will be drawing yourself out of the negative portion of the issue and creating an overview, looking from the outside in at the situation, your perspective will be lighter and clearer than it would be if you were emotionally drawn into the unfortunate, upsetting event.

Self-Control

Your body has several systems that work collectively to operate the functions of survival. You are the main operator because you have the freedom of choice. Choices are being made constantly, and some of them have become so habitual that you don't even notice them or identify them as the main cause for certain consequences you may be experiencing in your life. The law of cause and effect is very clear: every cause has a consequence, especially in matters of physiology. For example, if you exercise a certain muscle with enough resistance, then over time that muscle will eventually develop and become stronger (Cause = Exercise/Resistance, Consequence = Muscle Growth).

What you choose to eat on a daily basis has a strong connection with how you feel. Become very aware of the direction you are taking your body in. Exercise self-control when it comes to your diet, know your limits, and adjust your servings to get the nutrition your need, then stop eating after a certain point. If you cannot stop before you overindulge that means you are not in control. A few years ago, I was heading towards a weight-gain direction and I was not very happy about it. I decided that I would only eat half of the serving size I had pictured in my mind of everything I wanted to eat. It was tough to follow through with that.

I remember, to this day, a slice of white frosted coconut cake that was in the fridge. Boy oh boy, I wanted to eat the whole slice so badly, but I didn't eat the whole thing. I ate half and walked away. It took a few tries of practicing this action pattern to teach myself control over what and how much I wanted to eat. I did it. It was a very worthy piece of self-discipline I taught myself.

Another form of self-control for me is to go for months without drinking alcoholic beverages, even when a cold beer on a hot sunny day seems so appealing or a glass of champagne in the afternoon appears to be a good choice. You would be amazed how many people do not even realize they cannot go without alcohol for even a month at a time. Would you take the challenge? The point is having the ability to decline, even if you feel like it, so that you are in control. Make the decision because it is what is best for you, and not simply because the desire is stronger than your ability to make a conscious choice. When your desire for something overpowers your ability to decline it, it is usually an indication that there is a lack of self-control. Remember, your body is the instrument that reflects what you are within in order to act more precisely in the direction you must go. This is just one more reason why it is so important to know yourself, your core values, and your mission. Transform your life and become a better version of yourself. Your body naturally does it for you. Make good choices.

Exercise self-control and focus so that you think before reacting to events that trigger your emotions on a deeper level. We experience strong emotions at times, such as fear and anger, but if we practice self-control we can change our actions patterns to amend the outcome.

EMOTIONS

THERE are triggers for every emotion we feel. Emotions are signals sent by your body to communicate messages. When you cover up negative emotions with distractions instead of solutions, eventually you reach a boiling point. It explodes somewhere in your life or it creates an imbalance of overindulgent behaviors in order to overcome the negative feelings. Use your emotions; however, do not allow your emotions to use you. People get married based on emotions, wars start because of emotions, relationships begin and end due to emotions or the lack thereof, yet so many of us have only a small understanding of our emotions and we deal with them so poorly at times.

It costs us money, relationships, friendships, etc. Proper emotional understanding and emotional management, for a lot of people, comes naturally over time. Yet, for a few of us, it is an eternal learning curve. Make rational decisions based on rationalized thought processes; make emotional decisions when it suits the overall desired outcome. Know that, after the emotions pass, you will still be satisfied with your choice. I am a very passionate individual. I put lots of energy and enthusiasm into everything I do. Therefore, balancing the emotional charge behind my actions can be quite challenging at times. Nevertheless, I have made great development in this area. By adopting the measure mentioned above, I feel charged by the emotion and further rationalize my thoughts before taking action.

Self-control is a key ingredient to help balance that out. When I draw back from a situation that triggered a powerful emotion, and I allow myself to process it and understand the deeper root of it, I am able to respond more adequately rather than reacting purely from the driving force of that particular emotion. Instead of being used by that emotion, I use it to have a fuller understanding of why it exists and then I take the appropriate action. If you can fix the cause, chances are situations will not trigger your powerful emotions again in the same way. To be able to stop yourself from doing what you want in order to do what is right is a great form of self-control over your emotions.

How we react when we are angry or anxious, and what we do as a result of these emotions, has a direct impact on the habits we form and on the quality of our lives. People will react differently to the same emotions. While someone may scream when angry, someone else may take a deep breath and then calmly speak. Some people may eat lots of junk food when they feel anxious, while other people may choose to go for a run. What you choose to do, given the emotions you are feeling, determines how you start mapping your way through life. Hopefully, you have a good sense of direction towards where you are going, and even if you get a little bit sidetracked you can still get back on the right road. Remember to use your emotions and not allow them to use you.

You are in the driver's seat of your life. You determine which way to go. Do not allow your feelings to drive your actions, and your actions drive your habits, and your habits to drive your life, unless you are very aware this is taking place and you are happy with the results you are getting. Be the decision-maker and make good choices. Autopilot works well sometimes when you already have good habits embedded within you. But if you let your emotions, especially the negative ones, drive your life, then you will most likely reach a downward spiral that can even cause health problems.

How you label your feelings has a huge influence on how you actually feel. You can say "I feel a little upset about this" versus "I feel completely destroyed," or "I am hungry" versus "I am starving," and so on. Your tone of voice when you describe your emotions also has an impact on your feelings. Beware of the intensity levels you use to address what happens to you. Label things appropriately, and take some of the intensity away from negative emotions by using lighter descriptions and a calmer tone of voice when telling someone what happened. Otherwise, it could feel as though you are experiencing it all over again.

Sometimes a simple change of focus can change our emotional states. I just received a phone call from my young niece who's going through the emotional roller coaster of teenage adolescence. We had an amazing conversation about all the wonderful things she has yet to experience in her life. We talked about her coming over and visiting us for a vacation and all the fun we will have. I mentioned old memories from my youth in Brazil. Her emotional state after this conversation changed, and she was not sad anymore. Those are some of the change-of-focus tools we can use to move our emotions in the direction we want them to go. If I take myself to memory land, I can feel some of the experiences I had in the past just by thinking about them. Our brain does not differentiate for us; we think about a moment in the past, and suddenly the sensations are real within our bodies. The problem is that we are constantly thinking about past experiences that are negative, sad, and filled with frustrations and disappointments, and we are experiencing those feelings over and over again without realizing we have the power to change it in an instant. If we can change it enough times, then it becomes part of our reality.

A positive emotional state must be perceived as an emotional muscle that must be developed for us to bounce back when needed. We must keep pushing towards a continuous, strong, positive emotional state for most of the time. The best time to start exercising this emotional muscle is when you do not feel well. Acknowledge the negative feelings, then get up, wash your face with cold water, shake your head from side to side, and occupy your mind with something useful to you. Be in control of what is driving your emotions. Be in control of your thoughts and choose God's guidance as your main conductor in life. Ultimately, we search for a balance so that we can feel the feelings, the excitement, the passion, and the drive we need to experience a full life. We can empathize and sympathize better with other people if we understand and accept our emotions and feel our feelings. The key is to understand the signals our emotions are sending us. We must act accordingly, using the skills, tools and strategies we have learned to address them correctly.

FACING CRITICISM WITH COURAGE

ACCEPT criticism as a form of how others perceive you, not as a definition of yourself. You can grow and become better each time you are criticized. Take the hit, then let it go. The quicker you take those two steps, the quicker you free yourself to make a change or come up with an action packet to address whatever you were criticized about. That is a way not to take it personally. It is important to distinguish between what actually needs to be changed within you and what is just someone else seeing a flaw in themselves and thrusting it upon you. There was an instance where, in a six-month work review, my boss brought up all the negative aspects she perceived in me and my work. My response to that was to request for more of the negative so I could transform each negative point completely and become better.

It was uncomfortable to only hear negative things being said; however, I was able to see the bigger picture, which was the opportunity I had to improve even more. I did that and much more. I worked on my communication skills and I worked on not being so afraid of confrontation to the point that I would take certain treatments I should not be taking.

Please keep in mind that, in order for criticism to be of the constructive nature, it is best to communicate in a nice tone backed with good intentions, though it can still feel awkward to be on either side of the equation. There can still be love when there is critique. Focus on triggering the most probable resolutions and ask questions instead of making assumptions. You will amplify your good results if you embrace this attitude. Depending on how much one person is holding on to, and how much pressure they are under, certain forms of criticism can push people over the edge. Even criticism that is well-intended can break close relationships. Choose your channel appropriately, including the setting and approach. Not everyone has a thick skin or a soft heart in their life. We must strengthen our weak points so that we are not too sensitive to criticism, especially because what happens in the outside world does not have to have a direct impact on what we feel within, unless we have weakness we must fix within ourselves.

The versatility we incorporate into the different types of approaches to criticism keeps it fresh so that the person we are critiquing, with the intention to help them grow, will listen to what we are relaying to them. We tend to shut down repetitive modes or create an automatic reminder that they don't have much of an effect on us. Keep your critiquing skills sharp, and use different strategies, approaches, and channels with the final goal of overall enhancement, whether it is about the improvement and growth of your business, your personal life, or your personal relationships.

People will push your boundaries. You need to know when a form of constructive criticism is necessary. A lot of times, if you do not communicate your boundaries to other individuals, then they may continue with an action pattern they do not even realize it is harming you. You must do something about it. It is your responsibility to know where you stand, what is acceptable and what is not, and when someone should be treating you better and they are now. You must criticize them in way they can understand and learn to grow from. Your relationships can grow from adopting this behavior and viewpoint.

I understand sometimes we do not wish to risk losing a job, a relationship, or a friendship, so as a result we endure mistreatments and sometimes certain forms of abusive behavior. This goes on until we reach a boiling point or until we use escapes as a form of release, which do not fix the core problem. You can criticize so that you keep well-balanced relationships in your life. If a few people distance themselves because they feel as though you are not a good fit for their lives, this is a risk worth taking. It is a win-win situation: if they stay, your worthiness has been voiced and boundaries can be created from that point on both sides; if they go, you now have the opportunity to allow other people who value you and respect your boundaries to occupy that treasured space instead. Allow time to explain where you and the other person or group changed dynamics and stopped connecting and being of value to one another. Sometimes, time to adjust and take in criticism is what is needed.

If you have a good understanding of where you were coming from when you criticized someone, and you know your goal was a positive one, maybe the person on the receiving end needs to take some time for it to sink in and to understand and heal their own wounds. Additionally, if your channel and tone was not right, apologize sincerely, forgive yourself, and move on. Depending on where you are in your walk, the ability you either already have or can develop to pick yourself up from incorrect approaches, manners, behaviors, or actions, and quickly do your best to improve will be the crucial turning point for a successful critiquing world. Giving and receiving criticism is a part of life. Embrace it, learn it, and grow from it.

Staying True to Your Values

WHAT do you value the most? Why is it important to you? The answers to these two questions are of great magnitude. We are important, custom-made creatures, and we all have very specific instructions of who we are meant to be here on Earth. Staying true to our identity carries a meaning beyond our understanding.

Identifying what you value the most is an important step towards living a quality life, and especially living by your core values. What you value the most gives you an indication of what to choose or how to proceed in certain circumstances. Your decisions in life are best directed when in alignment with your core values because they lay a foundation for your overall happiness and wellbeing. Acting according to your core values gives you a strong sense of self-confidence. It is a form of internal reassurance that you are acting based on what you know, to the best of your abilities, from everything you have, at the moment of choice. I understand certain experiences in life may render difficulties. For you to stay true to the most original version of yourself, you must push beyond these obstacles. Everyone counts, and it is not what materialistic means we acquire that matters; it is who we become as individuals and what value we contribute to ourselves through our growth and ultimately to society on a small or larger scale, depending on what our mission is.

We are all part of this beautiful picture. We are the mega-pixels that give the color and the definition. At any given point in our life, once we awaken to who we really have become as individuals, we have the power through Jesus to change and to become a better version of ourselves. The

Bible uses the following analogy: "you are the salt of the Earth, but what is the salt good for if it has no taste?"

Obtain a clear picture of who you are. Remember, the clearer the picture, the better the aim. Move through life objectively, know your values and your intentions, and act accordingly.

Values and ethics are crucial in our business and personal lives. What we stand for and believe in, and are not willing to betray under any circumstances, lays a solid foundation, a base line to what our values really are. The bottom line is to understand what that is for ourselves and learn how to stick by those values so we can live a happier life. When we do not have a clear idea of our deepest values, we tend to break them and that makes us both unsatisfied and unhappy. We take two steps forward and five steps back, and sometimes we do not understand why. That is one of the reasons it is so hard to more forward quickly. Understanding your values and acting in tandem with them will allow you to move with confidence. Your decisions will be empowered and you will not be moved so easily by the unwanted influences around you.

SMILE

You have at least 60 facial muscles. Move them so that they make a friendly, approachable face. Smile, laugh, play. Remember, motion creates emotion. Smiling will increase your chances to create happy hormones that circulate in your bloodstream and generate good feelings of wellbeing. Try it right now: simply hold your front teeth together, push your lips until your front teeth are openly exposed, and hold it for five seconds. Now, notice how you feel. Exercise this motion until it becomes completely natural to you. Develop the habit of smiling. A smile can light up a room and smiling gives you positive feelings.

Smiling is good for you.

We all should smile more!

LIFE IN COLLABORATION WITH ONE ANOTHER

IT can be challenging to ask for help sometimes, especially when you are a very independent individual who works hard to achieve your goals. We must accept the fact that sometimes our mission is big enough, and it helps so many others, that it is necessary to accept a web of different forces working to make that mission come true. Humble yourself to this realization and balance your need for others. Make sure you always give to the same extent or more than you receive. Keep the give-and-take routine at the appropriate flow, in which each individual feels enriched from the experience. Live in abundance, and you will attract abundance into your life. When you give, you signal to your brain that you have more resources available; by contrast, living in scarcity sends the complete opposite message. Tap into the wealth provided by the wisdom within and you will always find the resources you need to accomplish your goals.

Know your boundaries and know the tipping point where, if you push beyond it, you will take away from your natural generosity that lets you feel enriched. Your balance must be at an equilibrium point and you are responsible for understanding where that equilibrium point is. Some people feel they give too much and they are constantly expecting something in return; so much so, that they do not realize it is coming back to them in different ways and from different sources, if only they could see it. Keep your eyes open to acknowledge the many blessings in your life. Be appreciative of the people who are contributing to your life in simple or complex ways. Say "thank you" to show the appreciation you feel.

I have found alternative ways to collaborate with others, such as through my writing and my video blogs. Sometimes, I collaborate by giving words of encouragement to others during a conversation or by being kind to someone during their time of need. You can collaborate with others by being loving, kind, or strong for someone else, or even by offering a word of comfort and encouragement too. When you feel you need something, start by giving it away first and then it will naturally come back to you.

Be the difference you want to see in others. Activate the source of abundance that may have been dormant within you. Change starts with yourself first, and then it expands into your reality and surroundings. We need to create the catalyst for the motion that ignites the journey. The best way to do that is through creating personal bonds with others. The motivation to connect with others must be deeply rooted in shared similar values for it to carry over long term. Work in collaboration with others, and you will see that your projects have a stronger drive that will last longer.

SET THE TONE FOR THE DAY

DECIDE to dress your soul in the morning to prepare yourself for the challenges of the day. Start by creating, or simply adhering to, a morning routine that empowers you. Morning rituals lay the foundation for how your day can potentially flow. You may need to backtrack a little and review your nighttime habits. The intent of this book is to help you create pathways in order to create a brand new life on your terms.

Adhere to the ideas and concepts that feel right to you. I have changed my nighttime routine in order to change my morning routine. It was simply not possible to fit in everything I wanted do each day based on my old routine. I started by assigning certain responsibilities to my kids, such as reading for 30 minutes every day of the week, taking online Portuguese lessons, and doing their homework by a certain time each night. This structure allowed them to know what to expect and gave them the initiative to accomplish these tasks on their own. Most days, I go to sleep about 30 minutes to an hour after they do.

I have also researched natural sources of calming. The teas I drink at night, when I am having difficulty sleeping, have been super helpful to me. My ideal morning starts by going for a workout, as I have mentioned before. I take some time to pray before getting myself ready for the day, and I use the time that I am brushing my hair or applying my make-up to think about how I want my day to go, what tasks I need to accomplish, and how I am going to accomplish them. Then, it's show time! I check my calendar the night before and, in the morning, I run a quick meeting to decide the course of the day. I try my best to stay connected. I believe God guides us throughout the day, and I like to be in tune with that connection and guidance to make sure I am making the right decisions and choices to keep moving forward.

THE GIFT OF ANTICIPATION

IMAGINE a huge rock sliding down a mountain and heading towards your direction. The anticipation of the rock hitting you straight on will probably make you eager you to do something. It is your choice to either prepare yourself by moving out of its way, or to react only after the rock hits you. That is, if you make it out alive. Throughout your life, there will be many circumstances you will be better off preparing for. Stop for a moment and take precautionary actions to minimize any undesirable outcomes. Write down a list of things you know you must prepare for. Keep this list close by and make changes as necessary by checking off items when completed or adding new items as you move along. Do something every day to prepare for the goals you want to achieve.

Do expect great things in life, but also prepare for the unexpected too. Try to focus on what you can do today that will create a better tomorrow. I like the "plan, organize, and execute" model. Beyond that, visualize what you want your life to look like and move your plan towards that. Common aspects of life to prepare for are as simple as budgeting to anticipate expenses: creating an emergency fund, acquiring respective insurances and protections, and preparing for your college, retirement, wedding, career, and investments. Additionally, you can prepare by creating an optimal daily routine for a healthy lifestyle, investing time and attention in important relationships to nurture them, and so on. Anticipation and preparation are two sides of the same coin, much like action and desired outcome.

GOAL SETTING & GOAL GETTING

DECIDE with clarity what you want to achieve in life and break it down into steps you must take towards your goals. Take action. If you want to live a long and healthy life, for instance, you must break this goal into smaller pieces by thinking about all the choices you make on a daily basis throughout your life. Educate yourself on how to become healthy and then do what it takes—not just once or twice, but every day. Eat healthy foods, manage the level of stress you allow your body to endure, and exercise. These are just some of the examples of the action packets you can incorporate for healthy living. The point is to do them repeatedly so you can reap the results.

Categorize your priorities by levels of consequences as incentive for what you decide to do first and foremost to the best of your abilities, and make sure you know the reasoning behind it. Understanding the reasons why you prioritize certain things over others may help you resolve any internal conflicts you may have in order to move more precisely towards your goals. Repeat this method of "Goal Setting & Goal Getting." Understand the consequences of your actions.

I have two kids and I was a stay-at-home mom for four years total. My oldest son was 4 years old when I started working. My young daughter was one year old. At that time, my decision was based mainly on how my time was going to be divided up. It was part of my value system to have either myself or their father taking care of them for the majority of the time. I valued that so much that we were able to work to achieve the desired result based on our priorities. You have your main set of priorities and value systems as well. When you make decisions, they must be aligned with your values; otherwise, it becomes very difficult to appreciate your life and to be truly happy. Remember, clarity and focus are great starting points for you to acquire the resources you need to live a fulfilling, happy life. Align your goals with your values and streamline them by making choices that will get you closer to reaching those goals. Working towards a goal will automatically increase your self-esteem. When you start seeing improvement and progress in yourself, that will excite you even more. In the process of "Goal Setting & Goal Getting," look at challenges as endurance mechanisms necessary to teach you something. Understand that, in life, you either win or you learn.

Technically, you only lose when you stop trying or when you die. Even then, there is a promised life through Jesus Christ, Amen. Make sure your decisions take you closer and not further away from what you really want. Adapt this decision-making process before every action you take. Quickly ask yourself the following questions: "Will this decision get me where I want to go?" and "Do I believe that what I am doing is right?" If the answer is yes, it will move you closer to your goal and it will not betray your core value system. You have the green light to go for it.

Discoveries and Contributions

You possess unique traits. There is no one exactly like you. You are original and unique, and your discoveries are of exclusive value to society. Over the years, throughout history, individuals have made amazing breakthroughs in their lifetimes. They have had the courage to pursue their core beliefs and dreams; and, as a result, their discoveries have improved the lives of many. Some of the discoveries and breakthroughs that stick out to me the most are: fire, the wheel, airplanes, telephones, computers, and the Internet. Find out how you can contribute to yourself by fulfilling your dreams, and ultimately you will contribute to society. Your perspective is important to the extent that you bring in a fresh approach, vision, or set of ideas that someone else may not have. Your opinion matters and your vision counts.

The realization of your endeavors is greatly beneficial to society. Refine yourself and allow your true self to rise up strong. Encourage the people around you to do that as well. Imagine if the great majority of people actually pursed their ideas with benevolence and if we all worked collectively in focus groups; then, think of how much we could actually accomplish compared to each one of us working individually towards several smaller goals. The difference is massive. If only the population would turn on the light of belief in possibilities and dreams, instead of simply living in a chaotic darkness. It takes each one of us to take control of our destiny by performing the action patterns necessary to get our ideas out of the ground and into reality.

We have the power to create, to imagine, to dream, and to make our dreams come true. Let's exercise our powers and bring them to life. A world of creative solutions to a better life is certainly a world more fun to live in. The natural revival of the belief in possibilities is crucial to our existence.

Performance in Your Every Day Life

The main starting point is a decision you must make about the direction you want to go in. Once you make that decision, charge each action with the energy and focus you need to pull yourself towards constant, never-ending growth. This will lead you towards personal improvement and accomplishments that you can have on a daily basis. Practice makes perfect. Do not allow yourself to feel as though you are dying while you're still alive. There is always a chance and there is always a way, for as long as you live. It is up to you to find it.

How do you balance the amount of time and energy you spend in each area so that you can expect the most return on your investment (ROI = Return on Investment)? This balance, if applied properly in correlation with your values, can bring lots of happiness into your life. For example, you value spending time with your spouse; however, you both have conflicting schedules and are only able to spend time together on rare weekends. This is a direct conflict between value and amount of time spent. As a result, your ROI may be diminished. Somehow, you must find a better routine that will grant a shared amount of time. Work + Time Together = ROI. Where your focus goes, energy flows. Your energy flows wherever you are spending the most of your time.

You must endure the training process first so that you can later enjoy the outcome. With enough practice, your actions will become your habits and your habits will form your new life. Transform your perception of what feels natural to you into a set of choices that enhance your life at every single level. Apply this concept into your personal life, your spiritual life, your work life, and your family life, and watch the transformation. Do what it takes today to reach this level. It is possible.

There are a number of skills you can develop in order to amplify your performance. You can develop the necessary skills to become a great conversationalist. There are many books on the subject. Or you can research public speaking, learn a new language, or even study how to dance, sing, or play an instrument. Every skill you develop enriches your own life and it also increases the number of things you have in common with others, making it easier to relate to them. Life is more fun when we share it with meaningful people. What skills are you willing to develop to become more relatable? Would you take dancing lessons? Would you participate in art classes, or take a photography class? Would you travel to meet new people and encounter different scenarios that broaden your horizons?

What books are you willing to read? What videos will you watch? How many times will you take a chance to practice the new concepts you are learning? Your performance has a direct correlation with the amount of time you effectively apply your knowledge. The more you learn, and the more your practice, the more your performance tends to improve until it becomes second nature to you.

GET IN THE KNOW

IGNORANCE is not bliss. What you don't know can potentially hurt you. Get in the know by educating yourself. Feed your mind with good literature. Expand your knowledge in specific areas of interest. Take it to a higher level and push yourself to improve the skills you must improve on. Advance your wisdom levels by accessing the highest source of intelligence available to you.

I was born in a small town in North Brazil. At age 13, I started taking English classes, but it wasn't until over a year and a half later that I could understand and speak English. It was surprising to me, because most of the time I would just feel completely lost during class; only, as it turned out, my brain was processing it all anyway. I learned from that experience that the repetition and collection of subject matter over time will compound into something greater.

Shortly after, I read "The Alchemist" by Paulo Coelho. The story fascinated me because the main character in the story was searching for the elixir of eternal life. This quest translated, for me at the time, to finding a way to achieve my dreams and to live a meaningful life of contribution to others. That was how I wanted to leave my legacy here on Earth. As far as the eternal life portion, being a Christian, I believe in the promise of eternal life and salvation in heaven upon Christ's return.

Once I learned English well enough, some doors of opportunity started opening up for me. Soon I began teaching English. My mother is a teacher, and I believe a lot of kids are influenced by the professions of their parents. I know I was. I started unlocking other barriers as well, like being able to read more technical books in another language (English) and then traveling abroad to learn a whole new culture. I was very much out of my comfort zone. I was only 19 years old when I was able to participate in an exchange program which allowed me to live here in the United States. Nowadays, I am so amazed by the knowledge you are able to draw out of yourself and enhance through reading, learning new languages, and understanding new cultures. Along with a combination of other factors, knowledge can take us far.

Networking with people from different walks of life is another way to get in the know. You can learn from them. Take into consideration that we all have a wealth of untapped resources that can be awakened at any given time. By networking, you open up your chances to either inspire someone else or to be inspired yourself. Be flexible with your approach and open to where a dialogue can take you. Adopt a clever way to be interested, instead of trying so hard to be interesting all the time.

Watch videos, movies, and documentaries with clear aims of what you expect to get from them. Be very selective over the information you allow your mind to fixate on by limiting your exposure to detrimental information. Ask questions to get to the deeper root of a subject. Do not waste any time. Wake up! There is so much to be discovered, enjoyed, and lived. Acquire the knowledge you need to appreciate your life to the fullest. Live a full life and experience the joy of astute living. It is fun, and hardly ever lonely. When you are in this state of mind, you are never alone because God is always with you.

APPRECIATION

I T feels good to be appreciated and it is essential to appreciate others. The expression of appreciation creates a desire to do more of what was recognized positively. A little appreciation goes a long way. You may feel accustomed to being treated a certain way or to having things done by someone else, so much so that you don't even notice the efforts of other people any more. If that is the case, then pay closer attention to what other people are doing. Giving positive reinforcement is a powerful way to allow excitement to flow into the constructive actions we want to see more of in life.

When you show appreciation for someone, make sure you are expressing it in a way they are receptive to, because each one of us may perceive appreciation differently. Certain people may feel appreciated when they receive gifts, while others may feel appreciated when you express your gratitude with kind words. Sometimes a simple hug and a big "thank you" does the job. Choose the way that feels more suitable to the individual and the circumstance.

Recognize the unique qualities of the people in your life. Make that the main focus and watch how they will light up with happiness. Understand that all of us have trials we are undertaking and, a lot of times, we may not see the outcome of our endeavors immediately. When you receive someone's positive feedback, it can be encouraging to pursue the same action towards someone else. This is a way to create a positive spiral effect by turning the wheel in the right direction.

Ultimately, appreciation is free and fulfilling to all parties involved. You must especially value the seemingly "small" things in your life; in reality, the big huge moments are very exclusive and sometimes rare, while the "small" moments are constant and need to be observed and highlighted as important pieces of your existence. Be grateful, and make sure to focus on your positive accomplishments in life.

STAYING CHARGED

WHAT keeps you motivated to complete your tasks and to fulfill your dreams? You are surrounded by successes and accomplishments. You must first acknowledge them and then build upon them. Look around and you will find many triumphs. Mistakes are easier to overcome when you are charged with a sense of certainty in the face of trial and error. No matter what happens, you will keep on trying, learning, and improving. Reward yourself to create a positive connection with pursuing your goals. You know, better than anyone else, how much effort and work it really takes. Make yourself complete first, and then, if others recognize you for your efforts, it will be a bonus rather than a necessity.

My daily connection with the Creator is my strongest source of energy. Love comes from Him and it flows out. When God is the main source of energy, He is an abundant source. However, when we try to get it on our own, it can be a great burden. I nourish this connection by praying, reading The Bible, and meditating in the mornings or at night before going to sleep. On Saturday mornings, I enjoy taking my family to the church service. I rest on Saturdays from all the activities that I have done, and I try to keep up my strength for all the activities that will follow.

Carefully create a vision of what your life will look like. Once you are working on designing your vision, the energy that it creates will fuel you during the tough times you may experience. It will be a pulling mechanism to get you moving in the direction that is closest to your vision. Call your vision into your life, using your imagination to make a picture in your internal visual screen. This is the part of you that, when someone describes a story, is capable of projecting the images in your mind as if you were there and looking straight at them. Use that same "visual screen" to project your visions and dreams.

Renew yourself by renovating your ideas and adopting a fresh outlook on things, or even by making a small change in your physical appearance. Mend misunderstandings in your life. Restart a project with a fresh approach, if necessary, or change your approach completely. Challenge what is for what it can be.

Another way of staying strong and energized is to quickly bounce back from challenges and to become stronger with each one of them you face. Ask yourself what lessons these challenges are trying to teach you and try to understand the adjustments you will need to make in order to proceed. You may need to acquire a certain skillset or fine-tune a talent you already have. You may need to learn how to be more proactive instead of reactive. If you adopt self-improvement as a constant practice in your life, then you will not allow adversities to block your way for long. You have extensive levels of intelligence and resources within you, so use all of these tools to keep yourself on the road to success.

Feed Your Basic Human Needs

TRY to understand what your basic needs are and feed them appropriately. There is a reason for everything. There is a very strong reason why your body and mind require water for healthier living. Drinking water is a necessity for our body to function well, and drinking enough water is a simple way to prevent fatigue and headaches. Water helps our brains and whole bodies to function well, but how do you know how much water is enough for you? This is a great question, and I highly recommend for you to research your recommended daily water intake based on your body mass index (BMI = Body Mass Index). Find what amount of water is right for you and be as realistic as possible, accepting it and applying it to your daily life. Remember, most things in life are not "one size fits all." You are unique; embrace it and get to know yourself on a deeper level.

Eat for fuel. Find the appropriate food groups that work well for you, and, if necessary, recruit the help of a nutritionist. For me personally, I have found that following a more natural diet works best for my system. My diet includes: fruits, vegetables, certain fishes, nuts, occasional meats, and eggs. I am able to keep up with the demands of the day, with my high-intensity workout routines, and with all of my home and business projects. I feel like the more knowledgeable I am about aspects of nutrition related to my body and how my body reacts, the more power I have over matching up the foods I eat with my corresponding daily needs and demands.

Breathe. Take nice long breaths throughout your day. Oxygen is another "basic," yet crucial, element for survival. I understand this is obvious; however, I would not state it in this book if I had not noticed how many people take shallow breaths throughout the day due to stress and several other circumstances. We should all be breathing more deeply, and purposefully feeding oxygen to our bodies in order to function well. Be conscious about your breathing.

Get some rest. The key question is: when and how? Make the time to sleep. Your body needs it. Build upon your resting time and design it for a purpose. I have removed the TV from my bedroom; instead, I keep a whiteboard listing my core values and my immediate goals which I erase and re-write as I move on to the next stage of each goal. I keep my reading materials next to the bed as well. I try to maintain a steady sleeping schedule, especially during the week days. Adopt rituals that enhance your sleeping time and let you wake up refreshed for yet another amazing day you must create. Relax your mind, clear it from any worries you may have, allow the calmness to flow into your body, and sleep. Soon you will be ready to get up and move again.

Figure out what kind of rest you need. Yes, you may need a break from something or someone in your life, a breather from a situation, or a timeout in a training session. You may need relaxation in the form of getting a full body massage, going on a recreational fishing trip, or maybe just having a good night's sleep or a nap every once in a while. Maybe you need peace within because you have been fighting for so long, utilizing the wrong tools, resulting in extreme emotional distress, etc. Or maybe your job takes so much out of you that you need to learn how to balance your work and your life. Perhaps a relationship fell through and you need some time to rest and to recuperate from that.

There can be a lot of reasons why you need rest. Address this need adequately after you identify each category you fall into, even if it is more than one or all of the above. Do something about it. Move your body towards a healthier and happier life. Prioritize the time for this by doing an activity that suits you well. Taking care of yourself is an important step towards creating your optimal life, and a great part of it is making sure that your body enables you to do what you truly desire.

Choose Uplifting Meanings for What Happens in Your Life

It is important to understand the underlying reasons why you are motivated to create a more solid sense of meaning within your life, which allows you to achieve the feelings of true happiness you may be looking for. The end of something you expected to be amazing, or life-changing, can actually be life-changing if you decide to give this meaning to it. It is not easy to change your frame of mind; it will take some mindful exercises. You have to know you are bigger than the challenge at hand. Even if you do not have all the answers, time has a great way of explaining it all. If you pay close attention, you may see it. Be strong in the knowledge that everything happens for a reason, and you must grow from each experience you endure.

It is vital to understand what effect you are truly trying to accomplish and to find healthy and sustainable ways to get it. Otherwise, you could get accustomed to receiving a dosage of emotional high and become a slave to whatever habit triggers that feeling. The side effect of getting a high from receiving texts or emails all day may be exhaustion. Imagine the quick excitement and adrenaline rush of receiving a new message thirty, fifty, or hundreds of times a day. The side effect of a romantic high is the possible addiction to that initial feeling of passion and the inability to develop interest after the initial "honeymoon phase" passes and hormones switch gears. In this case, a lot of times, a long-term relationship is almost nonexistent. The side effects of highs from certain foods, drugs, and alcoholic beverages are correlated with health issues, and so on.

First, let's recognize some of the most major triggers and analyze what long term effects they may have on our lives. Try to understand this concept and move past the motivations of temporary "highs" to find a more fulfilling and energizing way to keep a sound pace towards satisfaction in your life. Find a way that does not have a negative effect to you or your body in the long run.

Start documenting your ups and downs in a journal to help you narrow down what may be the main issues you are facing. Once you identify them, they will be easier to fix. Nowadays, there are many tools available for you can use. Smartphones can be a very useful tool for recording voice clips of your journal and the ideas that keep floating around your head.

Change your perception of something that may be bringing you down. Stand strong and give yourself the value you deserve. Respect yourself first so that you can also know how to respect others. Live, learn, and improve yourself, your capabilities, and your skills. Invest in yourself and in your own talents, knowledge, and life experiences. Be the person you want to see in others. Stop expecting everything from everyone else, and start being the first one who consistently brings something valuable to the table. Learn what your "standing ground" is, the foundation that shows who you are from within. Get well acquainted with that and build upon it.

Certain situations you may encounter in your life can be quite hurtful. Please know that, as much as it hurts, you can push through the pain or disappointment by changing how you label what you are feeling. Having certain dramatic reactions or giving certain labels to problems really does make things worse. Be aware of that. Choose your emotional labels wisely to ease the feelings those strong labels provoke.

Start Doing the Work Today

THERE is no better day than today to start taking the actions you must take to achieve your goals. Every little bit of time and action counts. Hurry, hurry! As soon as you build momentum, you will feel proud for not wasting much time. The sooner the better. Imagine one grain of sand in your hand; it doesn't seem like much. Now, look at a picture of the beach or the dunes; that certainly looks way more impactful and impressive. Or you can imagine one drop of water in comparison to the depths of the sea. Like a grain of sand or a drop of water, every piece of you has a purpose and a meaning and every action you take towards becoming a better version of yourself will take you closer to whatever that meaning may be.

The present time is a gift and it is to be used wisely. Why should you allow so many random things to rob your attention from the present, such as worries about the future or about what happened in the past? I know that analytical-minded people like myself are constantly trying to understand every detail of a situation, and sometimes we get stuck in that mode. The best way to build a future is by leaving a beautiful past; or, in other words, by doing the best you possibly can with the present time.

Today is the day! If you feel overwhelmed with the magnitude of all you see that needs to get done, if you feel like you don't know where to begin, begin anyway. Chances are, if you are in this stage, you may not feel like doing absolutely anything. If you are in this state of mind, and if you have made it to this portion of the book, that is a good sign. Whichever action you decide to take to move yourself away from this sense of being overwhelmed counts. The key is to keep taking steps towards clearing the mind clutter, and slowly this will translate into getting rid of the material clutter you may have accumulated around you.

If you are in a more advanced phase, you may benefit from designing your personal life plan and writing your mission statement. Start with your core values, and then move on towards your goals. It is important to have a plan. It is also important to learn how to bounce back when something does not go according to plan. Adjusting and repositioning yourself are key tools that will get you to your destination. Keep your eyes on the ball, aim for your goal, and trace your way there by taking steps towards it every day. For example, I weighed 145lbs and had 22% body fat, and my BMI was within range, when I first started training for my figure competition. My goal was to get down to 120lbs with increased muscle mass and 18% body fat.

With eight months of focused training, I was able to approach my goal. My weight got as low as 124lbs, which was close to my main goal. I had clarity of the current facts and I also had clarity of my objective. With the help of my coach, we set a workout plan. We were very consistent throughout the development of each phase, not allowing anything to stop me from training. At one point, we did not have access to the gym, so my coach found us a garage space with some weight training equipment that he had given to his friend after closing his CrossFit gym. We were unstoppable then, even training outdoors in the rain a couple of times. During the cold, snowy months, my coach would still knock at my door at 5:00am for our workouts. We were seriously committed to achieving results.

Adjustments were made along the way. There is a fine line between pushing through a certain amount of pain or muscle soreness so that you can grow and really knowing when it is time to take a step back, rest, and let your body heal properly. You must know yourself and be strong. You have to stand up for yourself and speak up when you are being pushed beyond your limits, then declare it is time to take a break for a little while. To summarize it simply, access the current facts, think of your desired outcome, and create and edit a plan to reach it.

If you still do not know where to start, perhaps it would be a good idea for you to do some more research in your area of interest or to talk to someone you feel may be insightful and helpful to you. You can also sign up for a class that interests you. There, you will find people that are in tune with similar goals and you will have a bridge you can build upon to create a bond with them. For me, CrossFit was that channel at the time of my initial breakthroughs. I was able to make one very influential bond that has generated a great, positive impact in my life: a friendship and a partnership with someone based on shared common goals. By combining our strengths, we were able to pursue some major projects together.

Make sure to stay true to your values and core beliefs throughout the searching process. Confront your fears and push against the barriers that may be holding you back. By doing this, you will create resistance over time. This repetition will make a stronger version of you the new norm. If your fear acceptance, work on accepting and loving yourself and understanding that we are all amazing works-in-progress shaped by our choices. Make good choices throughout your life and reap the benefits of them. The meaning you assign to the choices you make will carry you through the ups and downs during this process. Appreciate the journey.

MOVING PAST YOUR FEARS

So many dreams are yet to be discovered in the open when we move past our fears. Fear of failing, fear of hurting someone else's feelings, fear of being responsible for how someone else may use our ideas improperly, fear of rejection—fear, fear, and more fear. What if we were to trade our fear for belief instead? Belief that our actions towards achieving our goals will slowly silence the voice of fear inside our minds, until this voice is actually extinct. Belief that every step we take is being guided to carefully take us to a higher standard of living.

Fear paralyzes a lot of very talented people. It paralyzed me for a long time, until I wrote a declaration to myself—for myself—and read it out loud, asking to be released from fear. I asked God to forgive me through Jesus' grace, then I took a step further. I let go of the guilt and some of the fears that were holding me back. Those were just some of the first steps I took. Wherever you are in the journey, you must take the first step, then the second step, and all further consecutive steps in order to make it to your destination. Moving past your fears is an important step.

What if it all works out? What if your idea is a great and a fruitful one? What if all the work you do pays off? Choose to think of positive "what if's," because if you keep refining yourself, growing and building, something good will eventually surface. The most important part will be the process you engage with towards your vision that will feed your inner self and show you that you are living a powerful life because you are pursuing your dreams.

You must utilize the tools you have and fine-tune yourself. Remember to always do all you can do, and to give it your best. You can always maximize your chances by increasing your potential and your vision. The more confident you are, the less fear may strike. Look for methodical pathways that work for you and practice them daily. I pray a lot. I study, I read, I learn, I teach...Those are some of my personal daily action patterns that I use to strengthen my inner self. I have found the more I pray, learn, study, and teach, the closer I am to who I am supposed to be. That gives me a feeling of calmness and peace and accomplishment.

One of the beginning steps in my breakthrough, after the personal declaration for the release of my fear, was to make a change in habit. I adopted a new routine involving 5:00am high-intensity workouts. I started that routine shortly after our house was taken under a deed in lieu, which is basically a form of foreclosure, in the middle of the last recession. We spent our savings down to the last dime making our last mortgage payment. It was a difficult time for me. I do not necessarily blame the recession for losing our home, but rather my own ignorance at the time and some key financial mistakes I have learned to avoid. Since then, I have applied an enormous amount of time taking courses, reading books, and surrounding myself with great mentors in the areas of business and finance. This emphasizes the theory that what matters in life is what you do with what happens to you.

Do you get up, shake off the dust, and rise above it? When life pushes you around and throws you down, do you have the foundations to stand firm? We parted ways from our neighbors and moved a few blocks down our previous street to live in a nice apartment complex with a gorgeous view. In Colorado, beautiful natural scenery is everywhere, and I am very thankful for that. This apartment complex had a soccer field we could see from our back porch and a park surrounded by a nice walking path right by the river. It was recovery time. I had taken enough hits by then, and I was able to calm myself down and get focused again. Soon, I was offered a job I really wanted. I took the new job, and this new job brought a change of pace to my life. I had a more flexible schedule, which was helpful in coordinating my two kids' activities. I met an awesome group of individuals I worked with. They were strong-minded, intelligent people that I have learned a lot from.

Around this time, I started listening to motivational speeches instead of listening to random songs. Some of the first good ones I was able to find online were the talks by Les Brown. Once I listened to his material available on YouTube, I found what I was searching for. At the time, he was the best match for me. Try to know what you want first, and then find what fits best for you and what you are searching for at a given moment. Following Les Brown's material, I wanted to have more background with practical steps on the subject of discipline so that I could follow through with my projects. Then I found Brian Tracy. He has written an entire book on the subject, and I listened to the audio book online. That is how I learned that when you develop discipline, you do what you need to do whether you feel like it or not. I also learned that it feels great after you accomplish self-discipline.

All of that happened once I started moving past my fears. That is when I learned that God has a bigger plan and, if I listen carefully and rest in God's grace, He has and will continue to guide my life. I just have to pay attention and make good choices.

Within a few months after starting my new job, my work colleagues invited me to participate in the swimming portion of a triathlon. I had already started my morning CrossFit routine, and I had also registered with a local recreation center. I purchased my swimming gear and started swimming to prepare for the Triathlon. I finished in last place, literally, but I swam to the finish line across the 7 lengths of the Glenwood Springs famous pool without stopping. In the meantime, while I was pursuing all these new activities, I was learning that beyond fear there is satisfaction from hard work and achievement. The first few weeks of CrossFit were tough. My muscles were very sore. After the first day, I did not make it back until about two weeks later, but I kept myself invested and I slowly became more consistent. Three years later, I took a step even further. I increased my training in order to participate in my first figure competition as part of the National Physic Committee—the Warrior Competition in

Loveland—in the year of 2016, at age 33, after having two amazing children.

The point is, we must move beyond any excuse, whether it is how old or young we are, or even what has happened to us in life. If you have kids or a full-time job, like I do, or if you feel finances may be a setback when thinking about what it is you want to do, just do it anyway. First, get clarity of what you want. Then, you must allow yourself to become resourceful in order to get it or sometimes it will just come to you. The problem is that most of us operate in opposite mode, looking first at what is available and then choosing from that. We think "outside-in," instead of "within-out." When I go shopping, I like to know what I am looking for first, even if it is in a somewhat broad category and not down to the last detail such as color. My main objective with this example is to illustrate that you go searching for your resources when you know what they are, and when you know the reasons why you want them. Basically, the more you know about what you want and how it relates to you and the meaning of your life, the better chances you will have of getting it.

Make it simple. If you get tangled up in the details, or if you currently cannot even move past your fear of being disappointed, just take the next closest step you can, depending where you are psychologically. Resolve the internal battles first. Tell yourself, "Yes, I can. Yes, I am strong enough," every time your mind contradicts you by telling you, "No, you can't." You must immediately be aware and fight back, and a great way to do that is to replace that adverse thought that is popping into your mind and trying to push you down with a strong, positive affirmation. Clap your hands twice, shake your head, jump or play happy songs, just do not allow a negative thought that is keeping you from being resourceful to remain within you. Move right past that.

Understand that your problems have a great potential to teach you to grow. Understand that, in the face of adversity, you have an opportunity to make your perspective so great that it becomes greater than your problems. Now that you and I know this, let's do some of the things we are afraid to do. Use your life analysis technique to access what it will cost and how much potential gain you can end up with when you actually take the steps and do the work. How much time, energy, focus, and effort you spend working towards your goals will have a major impact on shrinking your fears down to size.

It will soon become so natural to you that it will become a part of you and a part of what you talk about. What a great trade! Doubt for certainty. Go for it. Go for it today. If you determine and follow a set course of actions, you will reap the results of those actions. If you live in fear, you will reap the results of living with that emotion. The best antidote to that will be deciding who you are and what you stand up for, understanding why, and taking steps towards it. Start as little or as big as you may be ready for. The key is to start and to repeat this process over and over and over again until it becomes a natural part of you.

Silence the voice of fear once and for all. Believe in the foundation you can potentially create by making good choices in your life. Have faith and certainty that there is a bigger plan, bigger than you and me, and we are a huge part of it. Embrace who you are and make yourself better every day of your life. Be curious about what is on the other side of fear. "Discovery" may be your new, longed-for word. All the frustrations that accumulated over the years when you were trying to hide who you really are, perhaps from yourself and others, are now out in the open. You are no longer afraid to express yourself and your values. You are worth it. You can make a difference.

Stand up for what you truly believe in and build strength to endure the consequences. Initially, the reward will be a sense of fulfillment. The biggest price of not fulfilling your role will be regret and disappointment, neither of which you or I should have to endure on our death beds. We must be the ones who stand strong in the face of fear, claim who we are, and work to the best of our abilities to reach the highest level of integrity. We work to refine who we are and the role we are meant to play in this world for the benefit of humanity, according to what God has planned for us to do.

Why should you and I take up this journey? The journey to be courageous, to pursue our true happiness, visions, and dreams. I know, for me, it is either pursue the journey or slowly die inside. What is it for you? Break the chains that are tying you down. Push against the walls of fear with every ounce of strength you've got. Walk one step further every day, past the darkness, and start seeing the light, the brightness of the sun and the stars, the brightness of joy and fun. Remember this brightness has to start within you and shine outwards. You can do it. Believe you can, and you will.

THE POWER OF CHOICES AND DECISION-MAKING

LONG for a clarity of mind that carries no burden within? Being connected to nature helps. Relax your mind and listen not only with your ears but with all of your senses to hear, feel, and allow the messages to really get to you. Listen to the messages that will connect the pieces of your existence. Our brains tend to naturally scan through situations to find problems; once a problem is recognized, signals are sent through our nervous system so we can react to it by moving away from what the brain has identified as a dangerous situation. This is a powerful survival mechanism. Just be careful you do not live an entire life of avoidance due to that. Learn to be a good systematic leader of your mind and take control over the recognized risks you wish to take. Practice a quick assessment analysis that moves you one more step closer to your initial reaction to a situation. Decide clearly what path you want to take and pave your way through it. Decision-making is a crucial step towards a more fulfilled life.

Practice decision-making and understanding probable consequences, including the consequences of not making a decision at a given time and, as a result, settling for the status quo. Become the commander in chief of your own life by taking control of your choices on a daily basis. What impacts your life will be the results of each of the choices you have made, whether you were thinking about it or not. Start thinking about it all today. What do you really want out of life? How many times will you have to make the same choice over and over again until it becomes a habit for you?

What new choices will you have to make to become the person you really want to be? Who do you want to have around you, and how much are you willing to learn in order to always bring value to their lives? How much time and effort are you willing to invest in yourself? What is the outcome you wish to reach? Make it a point to understand the answers to these questions so that you know what is truly motivating you deep within. You must embrace your personal power to be the leader of your life.

A very effective way to do that is by taking control of your decision-making processes. Decide today that you are not just a victim of circumstance, or just a product of your culture or society. Decide today that each time you take a breath you have a new chance to get up, to re-start, to rebuild, to reconstruct, to forgive, and to keep moving. Every breath is a new chance for an innovative perception of life, a new chance to dream even bigger dreams, and a new chance to use every experience to learn and grow and become better at life. Today is the day. It is time to wake up, and it is time to open your eyes with a fresh outlook and a renewed approach to everything that may have been locked up within you.

There are reasons and different motivational factors behind everything you have and do. If you have a deep understanding of yourself, chances are the majority of the things around you will reflect your inner self too. Some call this your "blueprint." If you do not know who you are anymore deep inside, you may be living a life influenced by external factors, such as the influence of movies, actors or actresses, influential business experts, friends, social media, or basically anything except what is truly authentic to you.

If that is the case, take back control. Start making some decisions today and follow through with them. Remember, you may have to make the same choice several times. I understand a lot of us are able to decide and simply move on. However, you may struggle just making the choice, and you may have to try again and again until it comes naturally to you. You have unique characteristics that make you special. The more authentic you are to your true self, the best-fitted you are to God's plan on Earth to raise you up and make you great.

So, creating a great brand new life for yourself and for other people around you will naturally benefit everyone. Every decision you make on a daily basis has consequences, and if you know what results you are trying to create beforehand, then your decisions will be guided towards those results. The problem is that a lot of us just aimlessly wander through life.

Our life goals are sometimes simply to "get through the day," "get thought the week, or month, or year," or "hang in there until the next vacation." Meanwhile, we are taking the present for granted and life goes on. We forget that, in order to get more out of life, we must put forth the effort to improve by taking the action patterns that will create the results we are meant to have. By that, I mean you have to work on yourself in order to grow. In order to have more, allow yourself to become more within first and strengthen yourself. Become determined to find a way and, if you cannot find one, make one. I understand it may not be easy depending on where you are in the process.

Please understand that the decisions you make will have a more meaningful impact on you when you are aware of your choices, aware of the reasons why you choose to do what you do. The key is to go forth, and if you fear, know that the only way to fail is to simply give up. "It is not over until you win," says Les Brown. It is important to follow the appropriate action patterns. Many people who are really successful at certain aspects of their lives have shared their recipes through books, media, talk shows, and conferences. Figure out where you are at. Decide what you want your outcome to be. Then look for the appropriate material, person, or guidebook that is right for you to map your way there.

The Bible is a great map that traces how to live a good life. Jesus came to Earth, and He has proven that is possible to live a righteous life. He has left many examples of how one should live. I could not simply recommend following in someone else's footsteps and leave out what I believe is the only way to the truth. That is what moves me, what motivates me always to grow and improve, to become a more refined version of myself. I understand that in this moment in time you may have different motivations. You can decide to read a book about your interests once a month, a week, or a day. You can decide to learn a new language.

How this might translate to you in your daily life would be the frequency with which you apply yourself to those activities and the results that are directly connected with your decisions and daily choices. Read or don't read? Practice the new language or do not practice? It is your choice, your decision. A collection of micro-decisions will make up your macro-results in life. The little things matter. Take care of the little things and the big things will take care of themselves.

Live one day at a time. Allow yourself to dream and envision what it is that your life will look like once your break through the barriers that may be keeping you on the opposite side of where you truly desire to be. You may feel you do not have much control over other aspects of your life and you may find yourself making the same old mistakes again and again and suffering the consequences. In this case, I actually recommend habit replacement: to exchange what you are doing that is causing a negative result with something else you enjoy doing that it is not harmful to you. If you are not working on your personal life structure, then you need to find out whose plan you are working towards and why? Because the time you spend during your life span on Earth is leaving some kind of trail behind. Decide to create a great brand new life today.

CONCLUSION

CHANGE does start and continues within us. We have an opportunity to create the lives we want to live. Nonetheless, the challenges we face on a daily basis either destroys us little by little overtime or we choose to overcome the toughest difficulties life puts in our hands whether is consequential or due to reasons we do not have an understanding of why. It is not easy most of the times, but it is possible to create and to live a brand new life. To have clarity is power and to take back control of the direction of the life we wish to live based on our highest beliefs and values. To treat the underlying causes over repeated negative habitual patterns instead of covering it up with momentarily rushes of emotions that fade away so quickly. To change us first and then if necessary distance others from us. To care and to be compassionate. To look at ourselves in the mirror and truly appreciate what we see looking directly in our own eyes and also appreciating our body image based on the self-worth and new choices that makes each one of us appreciate ourselves and others today, knowing that progress must continue because it doesn't matter where you are you can always get better.

www.ingramcontent.com/pod-product-compliance
Lightning Source LLC
Chambersburg PA
CBHW051433090426
42737CB00014B/2950